WHAT IS A CHRISTIAN?

Dave Jensen

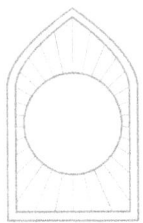 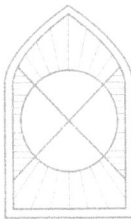 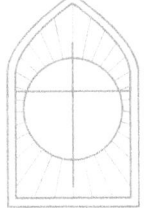

Republished and reprinted by Tron Books, 2026

Copyright © Virtual Church Assist Pty Ltd 2023

Cover artwork and design: Megan Hogarth

Previously published by:

Virtual Church Assist Pty Ltd

Bateau Bay, NSW 2261, Australia

First printing 2023

Scripture quotations marked NIV taken from the Holy Bible, New International Version Anglicised Copyright © 1979, 1984, 2011 Biblica. Used by permission of Hodder & Stoughton Ltd, an Hachette UK company. All rights reserved. 'NIV' is a registered trademark of Biblica UK trademark number 1448790.

All emphases in Scripture quotations have been added by the author.

Paperback ISBN: 978-1-917493-09-3

ePub ISBN: 978-1-917493-10-9

Contents

Introduction
What Is a Christian?

It sounds like one of those questions that should be simple to answer.

After all, Christianity is the world's biggest religion. Over 2 billion people on the planet identify themselves as Christians. It's possible that you've had some kind of encounter with the Christian faith; through going to church or interacting with Christians at school or work. Christianity is often spoken about in movies and media and in our society.

Defining what a Christian is should be a simple matter. Yet many people find defining a Christian actually more difficult than they first considered.

A Christian is...

How would you finish that sentence?
Often people say something like this;

A Christian is someone who...

goes to church.
believes in God.
tries to be a good person.
has faith.

There's always a contrast in the answers. Why do you think that is? Why is there so much disparity in how to define the core beliefs of the biggest religion in the world?

We have no problem defining other things. Someone who dances is a... dancer. Someone born in Samoa to Samoan parents is... Samoan. Someone who teaches mathematics to teenage students in a school is a... teacher. *So why is defining what a Christian is so difficult?*

Perspective

The answer is found in the word perspective. Perspective means how we see things. It's possible in life to be so shaped by your perspective that it makes seeing what's true very difficult. The mother who can't believe that their child could do the wrong thing, even when all the evidence points to exactly that. The fan who swears black and blue that their team is the best team even though they never win.

Because we all have our own experiences, interactions and exposure to Christian things, it can make what should be simple very complicated. We can be convinced we know what it's all about, when in reality what we know is simply the product of the way our perspective is shaping us.

So is it possible to work out what Christianity is about? Yes, we can. There is a perspective available which we can trust to be telling the truth. As the name suggests, Christianity is all about Jesus Christ.

Jesus was a real person who truly lived 2000 years ago. Most of what we know about Jesus comes from eyewitness testimony contained in the Bible. Whilst this provides the majority of information, it may be helpful to know there are also other non-biblical accounts of Jesus and Christianity that verify his existence and the historical reliability of the biblical records.

For most of his life Jesus did nothing of any particular interest. He worked as a carpenter in rural Israel. However at some point in his early thirties he entered into the world around him as a religious teacher.

He grew popular with the common people, but it didn't last. Around three years later he was betrayed, abandoned, arrested, tortured and killed.

He didn't write a book, no one painted a picture of him when he was alive, he didn't fight any battles and he didn't travel very far. He did none of the things we normally associate with influence or importance.

So what makes his perspective so trustworthy? To answer this question, we need to consider who Jesus really is. Understanding his real identity helps us work out whether he's someone we need to listen to.

Who is Jesus?

So who is Jesus? On one level you could identify Jesus by saying he is a carpenter, a Jew, a religious teacher, and a victim of an unjust execution. All of those things would be true. But how does Jesus identify himself?

'I and the Father are one.'
John 10:30

"'I am the Alpha and the Omega," says the Lord God, "who is, and who was, and who is to come, the Almighty.'"

Revelation 1:8

Jesus says he's not another religious teacher, or spiritual expert, or life coach. He says he is God; God's eternal son. It's what he says and does as God that forms the core of the Christian faith.

This means two things:

1. We don't determine what a Christian is - Jesus does.

2. His perspective isn't just another opinion, but the word of God Himself.

To find the truth, all we need to do is listen to what Jesus says. So what does he say? The answer is both the worst, and the best news you will ever hear.

Part I
God Made It

I

What Kind of Life Do You Want to Live?

Let's start with the end in mind. Imagine that you have a time machine and you're able to go forward in time all the way to the end: to your funeral.

You slip in the back unnoticed and take a seat. After a few minutes, the eulogies begin. Different friends and family members are eulogising you, talking about the path you chose, your work, your relationships, your qualities, your choices.

What would you like them to say about you? How would you want to be remembered?

Now think about it in reverse.

What would you not like them to say about you? How would you not want to be remembered?

You've only got one life. You don't get to do it again. It's important that you don't waste it. It's crucial that you live your life focused on things that matter. But how can you do that? There's no shortage of opinions, philosophies and ideas available for us to listen to. People have been discussing the meaning of life for as long as people have been discussing anything. Finding the truth can appear difficult.

Yet it doesn't have to be. If you're actually interested in finding out the truth about life and its meaning, you don't need to look all over the place to find what you're looking for. It's not a mystery for you to piece together.

2

God Created Everything

All you need to do is to listen to what God says. Why? Because he made everything. So he knows why everything was made.

Listen to how the Bible begins:

> 'In the beginning God created the heavens and the earth.'
>
> *Genesis 1:1*

God created everything. He is perfect, and creates a perfect world. The New Testament, written after Jesus, adds detail to the picture:

> 'The Son is the image of the invisible God, the firstborn over all creation. For in him all things were created: things in heaven and on earth, visible and invisible, whether thrones or powers or rulers or authorities; all things have been created through him and for him.'
>
> *Colossians 1:15-16*

It is in, through and for Jesus that everything in this universe has been created. The concept of this is staggering. Consider the numbers. The 100 billion galaxies, each containing a billion trillion stars; the 1 trillion individual life forms alive on earth alone at this moment, spread amongst 8.7 million species; the 8 billion humans alive right now, as part of the 100 billion odd who've drawn breath so far, spread across 24,000 people groups in 195 countries. But the most amazing number of all is one.

Despite the sheer number of people, the Bible tells us God knows each of us by name. He made you, and he knows who you are.

What does this mean? Take note of two major consequences.

1. The world, and everything and everyone in it, belongs to God. The world you live in is his, not yours. What you do in God's world, and with it, is important to him.

2. He didn't only create your life. He created your meaning. He knows why you're alive because he's the one who gave you life.

3

What does Jesus say?

So what does he say about why you're here? The Bible records an interaction that Jesus has with a religious leader about this very topic. The religious teacher asks Jesus about what matters most in life; of all the things God wants us to do, what is it? Listen to Jesus' reply.

> "'Love the Lord your God with all your heart and with all your soul and with all your mind.' This is the first and greatest commandment. And the second is like it: 'Love your neighbour as yourself.'"
>
> *Matthew 22:37-39*

According to Jesus, what matters most in life? None of the things that many people pour endless energy into; not money, property, reputation, success, or freedom. What matters most is...love. That's the meaning of your life. You were created to be in loving relationships. To know and be known. To love and be loved. That's why you're here. This is a statement that is evidenced everywhere in the world around us.

What Makes a Good Life?

In 1938 the Harvard Study of Adult Development began a study the like of which the world has never seen. They began following 724 people from a variety of backgrounds with the aim to discover what really makes for a good life.

Over eight decades the study tracked the same people and their families, asking thousands of questions and taking hundreds of measurements including brain scans and blood work. The second generation is now being studied.

The result of this study was conclusive. The researchers found one thing had more effect on physical and mental health (including heart disease and depression) and longevity than anything else: the one thing above all others that keeps human beings happier and healthier are good relationships. It doesn't matter if you're incredibly wealthy or impoverished, married with kids or single; the true richness of life is found in how we love each other.

Yet as helpful as this study is it was also unnecessary; as Jesus had been saying the same thing for 2000 years.

One Key Difference

However, there's one key difference in what Jesus said. He agrees that loving one another is crucially important in life. But it's not the most important thing. Look again at what Jesus says:

> "'Love the Lord your God with all your heart and with all your soul and with all your mind.' This is the

first and greatest commandment. And the second is like it: "Love your neighbour as yourself."'

Matthew 22:37-39

According to Jesus the very centre and core of your existence is to have a loving relationship with God. To love him with all you've got. This is why nothing else will ever give you what you are looking for; because you were created to find it in God.

Northern Irish author C.S. Lewis said it this way:

'If I find in myself a desire which no experience in this world can satisfy, the most probable explanation is that I was made for another world.'

What does this look like? We relate to God by speaking to him, in prayer. Listening to him, as we read his words to us in the Bible. But primarily, we are designed to relate to him by trusting him. Trusting who he is, and what he says about life and how to live it. Jesus says this is why we're alive. This is the meaning of your existence.

Part II
We Broke It

4

What's Wrong With
the World?

But it's at this exact point that a problem arises. Because even though God created people for love, that's not how we've acted. We have broken what God has given us.

The World Is Broken

The evidence is all around us in the world, in the way we treat one another. No matter what we do, humanity is defined by suffering; and most of it self-inflicted.

Consider the history of conflict. In the history of the planet, war has accounted for an estimated 150 million lives. 108 million of those between 1914 to today. The majority of the dead were not killed in combat but were unarmed civilians. But of course, it's not just war. Over 400,000 people are murdered every year, three times the number killed in war. Many of those people were murdered not by strangers, but by people they already knew. Why do you think that is? What would you say is wrong with the world?

The easy answer is to blame others. Often we point the finger at powerful people who abuse their positions for personal gain. Of course, that is a big problem in the world.

What Does Jesus Say?

But Jesus offers a different perspective on what's really going on in the world.

> 'Jesus went on: "What comes out of a person is what defiles them. For it is from within, out of a person's heart, that evil thoughts come — sexual immorality, theft, murder, adultery, greed, malice, deceit, lewdness, envy, slander, arrogance and folly. All these evils come from inside and defile a person.'"
>
> *Mark 7:20-23*

What does Jesus say is wrong with the world? It's not violence, hatred, oppression or murder. Those things are symptoms of the problem, but not the main issue. So what is wrong with the world? It's you. You're the problem.

The heart of the problem is the human heart.

5

We're to Blame

Because even though God created you to love Him, that's not how you've lived. But it's not only you, it's all of us. We've all said 'no' to loving God the way we should. We don't put him first in our lives. We don't listen to how he says to live.

Sin

The word the Bible uses to describe this is sin. Sin is a word, like the word 'Christian', that many of us find difficult to define properly. Many people associate it with doing 'bad' things, or 'breaking God's rules'.

But whilst bad things and disobedience of how God tells us to live are examples of sin, it's not the definition of sin. Sin is not about breaking rules. It's about breaking a relationship. Even though Jesus makes it clear that God made us to be people who love him with all of our heart, soul and mind, the truth is that we haven't.

To love God means not only to know he's real, but to actively listen and do what he says. But none of us want to do this. We want to be independent and run our lives our own way. We might say that God is in charge of our lives with our words, but our actions prove otherwise. All of us have actively rebelled against him. We all reject his love.

Sin Is Not About Rules, but Relationship

Imagine that you have a child. A very special kind of child. At school - top of every class. Best at languages, science, maths. Best athlete. The lead in school play. They are even voted School Captain in Year Eight! As a parent, is this a good child? Of course. This is the kind of kid that makes you look good! After school finishes for the day, it gets even better. They don't drop their bag, they hang it up. They prepare dinner for the family, do their homework, help their siblings, serve dinner, do the washing up and then tutor some underprivileged kids. They go to bed without complaint and have the lights off by 9pm sharp every night. Is this a good child? Yes! Amazingly good.

But there is one part of their behaviour I haven't mentioned. In all their life - through everything they've done they've never once spoken to you or acknowledged your existence. You congratulate them on school performance. They are silent. You thank them for cooking dinner: they walk straight past you. You go to give them a kiss good night, and whisper 'I love you'. In response, they roll over and ignore you. As a parent, is this still a good child?

No. Why not? Because as a parent what you want more than anything else is a loving relationship between you and your child. You'd sacrifice everything else to have it.

We're All in Rebellion

God created us and calls us to love him, but we don't. Instead, we rebel against him. Which means that no matter how well we behave or act; it doesn't undo the fact that our biggest problem is the rejection of God.

The Bible is unapologetically clear that we all sin. It's not an insult that religious people use against non-religious people, or that 'good' people make against 'bad' people. The best person you've ever met is a sinner. So are you. No matter how much we would like to ignore it and pretend it's not real, we can't, because it is and it destroys everything it touches. We see it everywhere around us. God tells us to love one another, but in our thoughts and actions we say 'no'. God tells us to forgive when people wrong us, but in our thoughts and actions we say 'no'. As a result our lives contain near constant conflict as we hurt one another again and again.

Why do we do that? We saw earlier that the problem is we're meant to love, but we don't. Actually, to press it even deeper, we do love, but we love the wrong things. That's what makes our rebellion so bad. We don't just make wrong rebellious decisions, we do them from our heart, out of love of the wrong things. For some people that results in lives full of murder, violence, assault, hatred, and rage. For others, it results in lives full of selfishness, gossip, pettiness, jealousy and greed. All of us play our part. Sin is at the heart of all the brokenness in the world.

6

Reality Check

Yet as bad as that is, it gets worse. All of those consequences are temporary and physical.

But the far more terrifying consequences of sin are eternal and spiritual.

Eternal Consequences

Our sin separates us from God. By our nature we do not know God. The relationship we were made for has been destroyed because of the way we act towards him. But that's not all. God is perfect. He has never sinned. He hates sin. Sin destroys everything good in his world. It has destroyed the lives of every person who has ever lived. It has brought death into the world.

To pretend it doesn't exist would be to make him unjust. It must be punished. The perfectly just God cannot overlook it. Jesus promises that there's a day coming when you will face judgement for what you've done in the life that you've lived. You will be found guilty of sin because you are guilty of sin. The punishment for your sin is the eternal anger of God, which the Bible calls hell.

The spiritual diagnosis Jesus presents is that when you die, you are going to hell. This isn't unfair or unjust. It's perfectly fair, and perfectly just. Yet it's also the single hardest truth all of us have to deal with. This is incredibly difficult for us to understand, because it is so different from how the vast majority of people think about life and death.

Scale of Goodness

Many people think about it the following way. Imagine this is a scale of goodness.

At the top is God. He's perfect. Down the bottom are the truly evil people. Hitler, Stalin, murderers and others. Where would you place yourself?

Most of us tend to think we're somewhere around... Here.

We know we're not perfect. We make mistakes. But most of us are not really that bad.

Now the question is *'where is the cut off line to be right with God?'*

Generally we think it's somewhere...

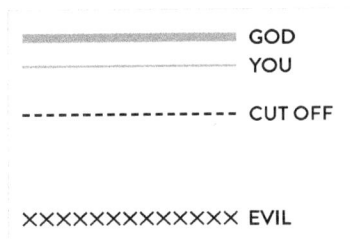

Just below us.

However, Jesus offers a very different perspective on eternity.

What does he say?

Being good can never get you into heaven.

None of your good works individually, nor collectively, are enough to qualify you for heaven.

Why not?

After all, if you want anything in this life you need to work for it. If you want good things you need to apply yourself and work hard.

So why does that not work with heaven?

For one simple (but very hard to hear) reason.

You're Not Good Enough

Being good can never get you into heaven because you are *not good enough.*

No matter how good you are: you are not good enough.

Of course, theoretically, if you could live your whole life with a perfect record God would let you into Heaven. He's a fair and good God! But that's just theoretical, because we can't do it. The truth is, we don't even want to do it.

Jesus tells us that our meaning in life is to love God and love other people with everything we have. Love God and other people perfectly.

It means the cut off line for God is not here:

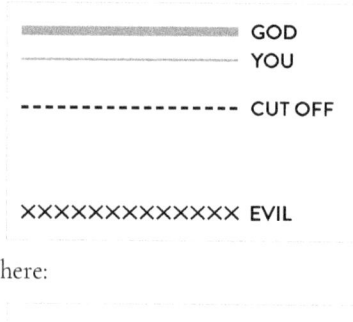

But here:

Perfection.

If we want to make ourselves acceptable by what we do God has said that the cut off mark is 100% perfection.

Loving God and others completely and perfectly.

None of us will make it.

Even if we were to be absolutely perfect in every way from now on it wouldn't un-do what you've done in the past. But no matter how hard we tried, we couldn't do it.

No matter how good we are, or think we are, we haven't done it. We've fallen short of the standard. And that's not all. Jesus says we will be judged not only by our actions, but also by our words and our thoughts. There will be nowhere to hide in judgement.

When we're honest about the way we truly think, speak and act, we know that the reality of our own spiritual condition is that we're not up here:

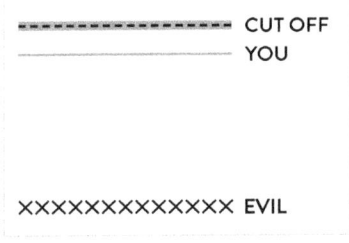

But down here:

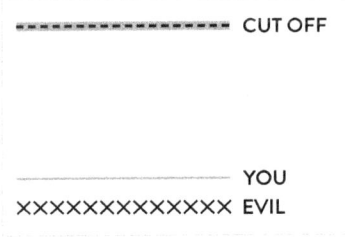

Not only are we not good enough for God, the reality is that we're not as good as we like to think we are. One day we will die and face Jesus in judgement for the life that we've lived. No matter how good we've been, it's not good enough.

God is perfectly just and cannot overlook our sin and pretend it hasn't happened. It has, and means we deserve punishment for how we've lived. Our sin means we are facing an eternity in hell.

Part III
Jesus Fixed It

7

Why Did Jesus Live?

But this is not the end of the story. We've already seen that the Bible reveals to us that we haven't loved God. We've rejected him and lived in deliberate rebellion against him in thought, word and action. But the Bible also reveals to us how God feels about us.

God Loves You

Despite rejection and rebellion, and a hatred of sin and all its consequences, God loves us. God loves you. He loves you more than you've ever loved anyone or anything. He loves you more than you can possibly imagine. Not because you're good, and deserve it, but even though you don't. So out of his love, God acted in such a way as to deal with your sin. He sent his son, Jesus Christ, to earth.

The birth of Jesus is celebrated around the world at Christmas every year, but it wasn't the start of his life. You have already read that he was there before the beginning, and that it was in, through and for him that everything was created. So when he was born as a baby it wasn't an accident. He came to earth on purpose. It wasn't the start of his life, but rather the start of his mission on earth.

Why Was Jesus Born?

The question is why? What did he come to do and how did he do it?

The good news is that this isn't a mystery for you to work out. Jesus tells you the answer very clearly. All through his life, Jesus made it clear that he was on earth in order to achieve two objectives above all others.

The first one is declared at the very start of his life. An angel appears not long after his birth and declares:

'But the angel said to them, "Do not be afraid. I bring you good news that will cause great joy for all the people. Today in the town of David a Saviour has been born to you; he is the Messiah, the Lord."'

Luke 2:10-11

Jesus Is a Saviour

Jesus is a Saviour, which is a word that means rescuer. He later says the same thing about himself:

'For the Son of Man came to seek and to save the lost...'

Luke 19:10

Jesus is a Saviour, who has come to save those who are spiritually lost. People who hear that like the sound of it. It's an admirable aim in life, to be a saviour. However his other objective shocked those who heard it.

Jesus Came to Die

Listen to what he told his disciples:

> 'And he said, "The Son of Man must suffer many things and be rejected by the elders, the chief priests and the teachers of the law, and he must be killed and on the third day be raised to life."'
>
> *Luke 9:22*

Jesus says he has come to suffer, be rejected, and be killed. But take note – it's not a prediction. It's not 'I will die'. It's a promise – I must die.

For around three years Jesus taught and performed miracles. He both attracted and offended large groups of people. His life and teaching was utterly unique and life transforming. But then it ended. He was arrested, tried, and sentenced to death. He was tortured, mocked, and then he was killed by crucifixion.

From a distance the death of Jesus looks like a tragic failure. The man who said he had come to save people – unable to even save himself.

8

Why Did Jesus Die and Then Rise From the Dead?

Triumph Not Tragedy

But when you read the eyewitness account of what happened you realise that's not what is taking place. This is not a scene of tragedy, but of triumph.

> 'At noon, darkness came over the whole land until three in the afternoon. And at three in the afternoon Jesus cried out in a loud voice, "Eloi, Eloi, lema sabachthani?" (which means "My God, my God, why have you forsaken me?").'
>
> *Mark 15:33-34*

In his final words Jesus quotes Psalm 22, from the Old Testament. Why would he say words which make it seem as if God had forsaken, or abandoned him? To point those who would hear to the reality of what was really going on.

Jesus Chose to Die According to God's Plan

Jesus's death was not outside of God's plan. It was God's plan. Jesus died at the will of his own father; and of his own will, freely.

Why? Why would God send his own son to death? Why would Jesus choose to die?

He died as our substitute. He died in our place.

The Book of Your Life

Imagine that your life story was written down in a book. Your name is printed in bold on the front cover. But this is not an ordinary biography. It contains everything. Every word and action. But that's not all; it also contains every thought. Every single thing you've ever done, written down on paper.

What would you do if your book was published and put on sale in your local bookstore? If everyone you know could finally discover the real you? When we're honest, we know that's a terrifying thought. Every person has done things we're ashamed and embarrassed of. Much of what has filled our lives is sin. We have rejected God and how he tells us to live daily.

The good news is that this won't happen. No one on earth can read this book because it doesn't exist. But God can. And he has. When we die, we will be judged according to what's in our books. We will be found guilty of sin, because we are guilty. God is perfectly just; so he must punish sin. He can't pretend that what you've done doesn't matter, it does.

Yet even though we've all sinned, God still loves us. So he sent Jesus to take the punishment we deserve.

On the cross, God took our 'books', and ripped off the front covers. He took out a permanent marker and wrote the name Jesus on the opening page. Jesus took our sin for us. As he lay dying, God poured out the punishment you deserve on his own Son.

Jesus experienced the judgement from God that you should experience for all of your sin. He died in your place.

The Resurrection

But it didn't end there. Jesus didn't stay dead. Three days after he was killed, God raised Jesus from the grave. He proved he is who he said he is, the eternal son of God, the one who created all things. He proved he is trustworthy, that when he speaks he is always telling the truth.

It also displays for everyone that the death he died was a pleasing sacrifice to God that truly paid the price of sin. Jesus fixed the problem caused by sin. He died for people who didn't love him.

After his resurrection, Jesus ascended to heaven where he sits enthroned as King of the world. He rules and reigns over all things. He is alive today, and in control over life. There is a time coming when he will return as God's judge over all who live in the world.

9

The Consequences of What Jesus Has Done

What do the death and resurrection of Jesus mean?

Jesus promises that one day he will return and judge everyone according to the life they've lived. All of us face condemnation from Jesus as judge.

Eternal Life

But it doesn't have to be that way. Listen to what Jesus says:

> "'Very truly I tell you, whoever hears my word and believes him who sent me has eternal life and will not be judged but has crossed over from death to life.'
>
> *John 5:24*

Because of his death in your place he now offers to forgive all of your sins. The punishment you deserve has been paid for. Jesus commands everyone, everywhere, including you, to stop rebelling against him. To turn back to him and trust him.

Trust him how?

As your Saviour: To stop depending on your own works to justify yourself before God for the life to come, and instead to trust in the death and resurrection of Jesus for your salvation. Your sins have been paid for.

As your King: To stop rebelling against him and turn back and obey him as your master in your life. To follow him in life, choosing to obey what he says.

If you do so Jesus promises that you will enter into a loving relationship with God, which starts now and lasts forever. Listen to what he says;

'Now this is eternal life: that they know you, the only true God, and Jesus Christ, whom you have sent.' *John 17:3*

Conclusion

What Is a Christian and How Do You Become One?

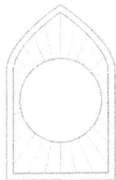  

God Made It   We Broke It   Jesus Fixed It

Many people believe that a Christian is someone who... goes to church, believes in God, tries to be a good person, has faith.

Those are important things to do as a Christian. Yet the perspective Jesus gives us makes it clear that you can do all of those things and still not be a Christian. Why?

Because being a Christian is not about 'what I do'. It's about 'what Jesus has done for me'. He died on the cross and rose from the dead to take the punishment for your sins and conquer death.

So... what is a Christian?

A Christian is someone who has been saved by Jesus to follow Him as their King.

How Do You Become a Christian?

You become a Christian by accepting the sacrifice Jesus has made on your behalf. In other words you turn from the rebellious way you've been living, and actively trust in what Jesus has done.

When you do so Jesus promises that God has forgiven your sins, and granted you eternal life. He enters into a relationship with you. He gives you the Holy Spirit, God himself, to live within our hearts and help us continue to follow him. He speaks to us, in his word the Bible, and we can speak to him in prayer. We get to gather with fellow Christians to worship God together and encourage each other as we follow Jesus.

That is what a Christian is.

Are You a Christian?

The question is: *Are you a Christian?*

If Jesus is not your Saviour and your King, then the answer to that question must be 'no'.

However, it is not too late. You can become a Christian, right now. In fact, it might be possible that God is inviting you to do so this very moment.

The way to do so is to simply talk to God in prayer. You could pray something like this:

Dear God,

I realise I have rebelled against you, in thought, word and deed. I am a sinner. I'm sorry I've done this, and ask you to forgive me.

I know that Jesus died on the cross to take the punishment I deserve. I know that if I trust in him you have forgiven me. Thank you that he rose from the dead to give me new life.

As best I can, and with your help Father, I will turn away from rebellion and follow Jesus as my King.

Please come into my life and take complete control of it.

Amen.

If you would like to become a Christian, why don't you pray that prayer right now?

If you did, the Bible tells us that heaven celebrates every time one of God's children comes home to him. But this isn't the end of your spiritual journey, it's just the beginning.

Whether you have or haven't put your trust in Jesus, there are three things that you can do now that will be great next steps.

The best thing you can do now is read about Jesus for yourself in one of the four biographies of his life that are in the Bible. The Gospel of Mark is a great place to start. If you don't have a Bible you can go to biblica.com/bible.

Secondly, visit a Bible believing church near where you live.

Finally, speak to a Christian that you know about what you've read.

WHY
WE
PRAY

William J U Philip

'Internalise these great Bible truths and
your prayer life will come alive.'
Rico Tice

TRON BOOKS

Prayer is foundational to the Christian life, but many people don't understand it. What is it for? How does it work? Why do we do it? This short and accessible book explains what prayer is, why it exists and how it can encourage us in our life of faith.

Written by a pastor with years of teaching and counselling experience, Why We Pray doesn't simply tell readers why they should pray, but instead focuses on four blessing-filled reasons that will help us want to pray. Rather than feeling discouraged and disheartened by our inconsistency in prayer, we feel reinvigorated to approach God with confidence and joy, delighted by the privilege of talking directly to our heavenly Father.

The TRON Church

Our church is part of the worldwide family united by the cross of Jesus. Students, young workers, families and older saints, from many nationalities and all walks of life – we are all one in Christ Jesus.

Our vision, which drives everything we do, is to see the risen Lord Jesus crowded by people from our city and every nation, ransomed by his blood and raised by his Spirit through the gospel, reigning for eternity with him to the glory of God the Father.

So we worship together to make and grow mature disciples of Jesus Christ in ever greater numbers who with us will glorify God and enjoy him forever.

We are a presbyterian church and are committed and accountable to a wider family of congregations in Scotland called the Didasko Presbytery.

If you are visiting Glasgow, do be sure to visit us on a Sunday. For more information, visit our website - tron.church

TRON BOOKS

Launched in 2024, Tron Books seeks to produce and distribute excellent Christian books that both equip and encourage church leaders and members. Our hope is to publish a range of biblically-faithful, stimulating and timeless publications that will help those in the pulpit or pew to prosper in their Christian walk and service.

To find out more, visit our website - tron.church/books

MADE ALIVE
PRESS

Made Alive Press exists to publish Christian resources shaped by one central conviction: that God brings life through his Word. The Bible teaches that people are spiritually dead by nature, yet made alive together with Christ through the gospel of Jesus. Everything we produce is designed to clearly present Jesus to those who do not yet know him, calling people from death to life, and to strengthen believers as they grow in that new life. We publish with one purpose: that through clear, faithful words, God would save, transform, and sustain his people.

www.ingramcontent.com/pod-product-compliance
Ingram Content Group UK Ltd.
Pitfield, Milton Keynes, MK11 3LW, UK
UKHW060659230326
11423UKWH00029B/137